THE FULFILLED MARRIAGE

by

Norman Wright

Harvest House Publishers
Irvine, California 92714

FULFILLED MARRIAGE

© 1976 by Harvest House Publishers,
Irvine, CA 92714
Library of Congress Catalog Card
Number 76-21981
ISBN 0-89081-060-5

Printed in the United States of America.

THE FULFILLED MARRIAGE

"My marriage would be a whole lot better if only . . ." Have you ever heard that statement? Have you ever said it—or thought it? Many people have. This statement reflects two very common facts of married life: (1) people want more than they are getting from their marriages; but (2) they use excuses and blame others for the less-than-ideal state of their marriage.

When a marriage isn't the way a person wants it, the excuses abound. Blaming others for one's problems or circumstances is a common human failing. When people have difficulty in marriage they seem to resort to two procedures: they defend themselves and they try to discover why the other person does what he does. They think they'll be happy when they know why the other person acts as he does. However, knowing why a person does something doesn't necessarily solve the problem. It isn't always important to find out why, nor is it always possible. What is important is to spend time determining what is going on in a relationship and making plans for solving the difficulties or making the necessary changes. Reasons may be important at times, but too often they are used as excuses!

Let's look at some typical excuses that people use when they consider why their marriage isn't what they want it to be.

Some people blame their health.
I've had this cold for three months now . . .
I have migraine headaches and . . .
I'm just tired all the time . . .
My metabolism is just different from yours . . .

Some people blame their feelings.
My nerves are so shaky, and you don't help them at all . . .
I've been depressed . . .
The kids make me so upset . . .

Some people blame their nature.
I'm just this way, that's all. I always have been.
I can't change.
I am a phlegmatic—you know what they're like . . .

Some people blame others.
Her mother is always . . .

His boyfriends are really . . .
It's the darn kids. They just never go to sleep at the right time . . .
My boss just gets to me. And then . . .

Some people blame the past.
She has always been that way . . .
Nobody has ever liked me and they never will . . .
My other marriage was lousy too . . .
My mother always used to put me down . . .

Some people blame their partners.
He makes me so upset I could scream . . .
If only she'd shut up and listen to me . . .
He's an animal. All he thinks about is food, TV, and sex, and not in that order either!
If she'd ever clean the house I'd faint.
If only she'd be a little neater around the house . . .
If she'd fix herself up, then I might give her some attention.
If she'd only go to cooking school and learn to satisfy my stomach we'd have a decent marriage.
If she would read some books once in a while and stretch her mind then we could talk and discover something in common!

Some people blame "why."
Why we don't communicate . . .
If I could only understand why he does . . .
But why can't he stay home on Saturday nights . . .

Excuses accomplish only one thing—they keep you from really working on your marriage. *When you stop thinking about what you can't do and why you can't do it, and begin to think about what you want from marriage and what you can do to get it, then your marriage will begin to be what you want it to be!*

Many people feel that their own behavior and the progress of their marriage depend upon how their partner behaves and upon the circumstances of life. Not so! If you find yourself blaming your spouse or your circumstances for all of your difficulties and problems, you had better look for a new approach. It would be difficult to pick a *worse* method for building the type of marriage that you're looking for!

Is this what you expected to read when you picked up this book? If not—why not read on? This book will show you, step-by-step, how to enrich your marriage. *It is possible to have a fulfilling marriage that meets the needs of both partners and allows each to develop his or her potential and to bring glory to God!*

This book is not like many of the other books on marriage, for you cannot just read it—you must react to it, talk to it, argue with it and act upon it. You will be asked to evaluate your present role in your marriage and to make changes. You'll be asked to think! To plan! To grow!

Remember: it will take hard work and lots of effort to make a marriage grow. If what you have been doing hasn't been working, why not try a new approach? What have you got to lose?

Let's look at the steps you can take to enrich and enhance your marriage.

Identify your expectations for marriage; compare them with the actual purpose of marriage.

When you married you had a number of expectations and dreams concerning your marriage relationship, your spouse, and your life style. Did you ever share these dreams and expectations with your spouse and ask what his or her expectations were? What does your spouse expect from the marriage relationship right now? What does he or she expect from you as a marriage partner? Write down what you think your partner would say; then ask for his or her response.

My spouse's expectations from marriage are:

____

____

____

____

My spouse's expectations from me are:

____

____

____

____

My expectations from marriage are:

____

____

____

____

My expectations from my spouse are:

____

____

____

____

When you came into your marriage you brought a whole set of values and expectations that you had developed from observing your parents and from your lifetime of experiences. Your spouse brought another set of values and expectations. These may differ. You may find that you and your partner expect different things from marriage. You have now compared your expectations with those of your spouse, so let's look at your *ideal* of marriage. Answer the following questions on a separate piece of paper. Get your mate to do the same; then discuss your answers.

<u>MY IDEAL MARRIAGE</u>

Wife's Thoughts	*Husband's Thoughts*

How would you have described the
ideal marriage ten years ago?

How would you describe an ideal
marriage for you now?

What led you to change your ideas about
an ideal marriage (if they changed)?

Describe what your marriage will
be like in five years.

It has been said that the process of
marriage introduces a world full of pictures.
The selection of your mate was marked by
dreams and expectations which filled you
with anticipation. The success or failure of
your marriage, however, often depends upon
your ability to survive disappointments or to
readjust your dreams to fit reality.[1]

1. Harnick, Bernard. *Risk and Chance in Marriage*. Waco,
   Texas: Word Books, 1972, p. 17.

The marriage relationship is a school, a learning and growing environment in which (if everything is as it should be) both partners can grow and develop. The relationship grows along with them. If you can see marriage as an opportunity for growth you can be satisfied and can satisfy your spouse.

Dr. David Hubbard graphically described the marriage relationship when he said, "Marriage does not demand perfection. But it must be given priority. It is an institution for sinners. No one else need apply. But it finds its finest glory when sinners see it as God's way of leading us through his ultimate curriculum of love and righteousness.[2]"
Have you ever thought about the purpose of marriage in that light before?

Here's another definition of marriage. Consider it carefully, and then talk over your feelings with your partner: "A Christian marriage is a total commitment of two people to the person of Jesus Christ and to one another. It is a commitment in which there is no holding back of anything. Marriage is a pledge of mutual fidelity, it is a partnership of mutual subordination. A Christian marriage is similar to a solvent, a freeing up of the man and woman to be themselves and

2. From a message by Dr. David Hubbard, President of Fuller Theological Seminary.

become all that God intends for them to become. Marriage is a refining process that God will use to have us become the man or woman He wants us to become."

Think about it. God will use your marriage for His purpose. He will mold and refine you for your own benefit and for His glory.

Read again the last sentence in the definition of marriage: "It is a refining process that God will use to have us become the man or woman He wants us to become." God will allow the unexpected to happen in your marriage so that you may grow. You may not like some of the things that happen. You may not enjoy the loss of a home or a job, the cancellation of a vacation, or the fire that destroys your keepsakes and wedding pictures. You may question the wisdom of God in the death of a child or the permanent disability of your spouse. *How you respond to these unexpected events in your marriage will determine whether you and your marriage grow or how they are destroyed!* If you realize that the purpose of marriage is to allow God to develop you, your attitude toward the unexpected events of life will allow you to grow. You may wish that a certain thing had never happened, but you can't change it. You can honestly say, "If I were God I don't think that I would have allowed this to happen. But since it *has* happened, what can I learn from it? How can I grow and change because of it? How can God be glorified through this?" You can have this attitude—or you can allow what the world calls tragedies to destroy and cripple you emotionally and eventually put such a damper on your marriage that nothing but pain is left.

My wife and I have had to learn to look to God in the midst of seeming tragedy. We have two children, a daughter, Sheryl, who is fifteen, and a son, Matthew, who is nine. Mentally, however, Matthew is at about a two-year-old level. He is a brain-damaged, mentally retarded boy who may never develop past the three-year-old level mentally. Matthew can walk but he cannot talk or feed himself; he is not toilet trained. He is classified as severely retarded.

We did not anticipate becoming the parents of a mentally retarded son. But Matthew is ours. And we have learned and grown through the process of caring for him. I have been an impatient, selfish person in many ways. But because of Matthew I have learned to be more patient. When you wait for a child to be able to reach out to handle an item; when you wait for three or four years for him to learn to walk, you develop patience. We have had to learn to be sensitive to a person who cannot communicate his needs, hurts or wants verbally. We must decipher what he is trying to say; we must interpret his nonverbal behavior. Needless to say we have grown through this process. We have experienced times of hurt, frustration, sorrow and pain. But we have rejoiced and learned to thank God for progress that we ordinarily take for granted. The meaning of the word Matthew, which is "God's Gift" or "Gift from God" has become very real to us. We could have let our son's problem embitter and confuse us and thus hinder our growth as individuals; we could have let it become a source of estrangement in our marriage. But instead we have grown and developed through this experience.

The attitude that a person has toward the difficulties of life will make the difference in how he is affected by them. We can say, "This certainly is not what I planned, but since it has happened, Lord, what should I do? What can I learn through this event?"

My wife and I also discovered something else about the way God works. We realized that God had prepared us for Matthew's coming even years before, though we hadn't realized that the preparation was taking place. We believe that this is true for others, too. In our case, when I was in seminary I had to write a thesis. Not knowing what to write about, I asked one of my professors for suggestions. years later I realized that she was the first one that God used to begin the preparation. She assigned me my thesis title—"The Christian Education of the Mentally Retarded Child." I knew absolutely nothing about it. But I learned in a hurry. I read books, went to classes, observed training sessions in hospitals and homes, and finally wrote the thesis. I rewrote it three times and my wife typed it three times before it was accepted.

Later on, my graduate studies in psychology required several hundred hours of internship in a school district for the school psychologist training. The school district I was in assigned me the task of testing the mentally retarded children and placing them in their respective classes.

While serving as a minister of education in a church for six years, I was asked by the church board to develop a Sunday school program for retarded children. My duties included developing the ministry and the curriculum and training the teachers.

Two years before our son was born, my wife, Joyce, and I were talking one evening. One of us said, "Isn't it interesting that we are having all of this exposure to and learning so much about retarded children. Could it be that God is preparing us for something that is going to occur later on in our life?" That is all we said at the time. I can't even remember which one of us said it. Two years later Matthew was born; eight months after that his seizures began. The uncertainty that we had felt over the rate of his progress was now a deep concern. Thus we learned of our son's condition and we began to see how the Lord had prepared us.

When you encounter any type of difficulty in your marriage, either individually or as a couple, ask yourself, "How has God prepared me for this?" He has, even though you may not know it at the time. You will discover that the resources to handle what is happening in your life are available either through advance preparation or through God's provision at the time of the need. You will discover anew the scripture, "My grace is sufficient for you" (II Cor. 12:9, RSV).

Develop a balanced love response toward your spouse.

Most people in our country do not understand the meaning of the word "love;" they equate it to a strong emotional or visceral response. If the emotional pounding of the heart and the activation of the glandular system are absent, some doubt the validity of their love for the other. An emotional response is nice, but its presence does not necessarily mean love. The purely emotional idea of love is summed up in this statement: "Love is a feeling you feel when you get a feeling you've never felt before."

Love is more than a feeling. Love is an unconditional commitment to an imperfect person. When we have this attitude a new sense of realism enters the marriage and makes growth possible. Love is an inner commitment; it is knowing you love even when you don't *feel* it. To love somebody is not just a strong feeling—it is a decision, it is a judgment, it is a promise.[3] There may be times when you have little or no feeling, but you know that you love the other person. And this love can be deepened and enhanced emotionally by your behaviors toward your spouse. Edward Ford said, "It is in the very process of doing things for others that you begin to fall in love. It is in the very process of doing things with and for others that you stay in love.[4]"

3. Fromm, Erich. *The Art of Loving.* New York: Harper & Row, 1956, p. 56.

4. Ford, Edward. *Why Marriage?* Niles, Ill. Argus Publishers, 1974, p. 58.

Look at all of the little actions which seemed to be so essential when you dated—the gifts, the compliments, the loving touches. Where are they now? Why the routine and the ruts that we dig for ourselves? Make a list of the loving actions that you and your spouse used to enjoy. Put them back into practice. These are important in nurturing your love for one another. When love is not practiced in action and in words, an insidious, deadly disease begins to invade the relationship—indifference. "The tragedy of love is not death or separating, but the tragedy of love is indifference.[5]"

Respond to your spouse first as a fellow Christian—a friend—and then as your mate.

If you would respond to your spouse as a fellow Christian first, putting into practice the scriptural teaching for this kind of relationship, and then add to it the element of married love, what would that relationship be like?

5. Maugham, Somerset. *The Trembling of a Leaf.* New York: George H. Doran Co., 1921, Chapter 4.

One of the greatest disasters to hit marriage is thinking of the spouse as a lover and sexual partner without seeing him or her as potentially the greatest friend one could ever have. Marriage is a form of friendship—it is a gift from God. Do you know what the elements of friendship are? James H. Olthuis in his book *I Pledge You My Troth* has given a beautiful description:

"Friendship is reciprocal, preferential, and selective. Friendship is a pledged vow of troth between two persons based upon psychic congeniality.

"Friendship is exuberant, spontaneous, and tender. Friends support one another and count on one another; they even begin to think alike. A friend can be called on for help, but we are almost embarrassed to trouble him in this way. For when a friend sees a problem, he offers help, but he doesn't want it mentioned. He only did what a true friend does. No one deliberately treats a friend shabbily, but he understands when we do. We treasure a good friend. When we say to ourselves, 'He is worth his weight in gold,' the old cliche takes on real meaning for us. A person has only a few such friends, if that many, in his entire life. As Francis Bacon exclaims, a friend 'doubles a man's joy and cuts his sorrow in half.'

"On the other hand, a friend says his piece;

he doesn't automatically approve of everything we do or say, and we take it because we know it is for our own good. As Solomon put it, 'Faithful are the wounds of a friend; but kisses of an enemy are deceitful' (Prov. 27:6, KJV). Face to face and heart to heart friends affect each other and grow. 'Iron is made the finer by iron,' exclaims Proverbs 27:17 (JB), 'man is refined by contact with his neighbour.' Friendship involves mutual confidence, trust, effort and devotion.

"Friends do not attempt to control each other because they respect each other too much. Friends give themselves, for only in mutual self-giving can trust and friendship prosper. Holding back in order to control the situation and manipulate a friend kills troth and deepens loneliness. Friends can accept anything from each other—except a break in troth. The only injury to a friend is mistrust, which will end the friendship if it is not corrected. Ecclesiasticus says it beautifully:

> If you have drawn your sword on a friend,
> do not despair; there is a way back,
> If you have opened your mouth against
> your friend, do not worry; there is hope
> for reconciliation;
> But insult, arrogance, betrayal of secrets,
> and the stab in the back—

> in these cases any friend will run
> away.
> (Eccles. 22:21-27, JB)

David makes the same point:
> Were it an enemy who insulted me,
>   I would put up with it;
> Had a rival got the better of me,
>   I could hide him.
> But, you, a man of my own rank,
>   a colleague and a friend,
> To whom sweet conversation bound me
>   in the house of God! (Ps.55:12-14, JB).[6]"

Be accepting and understanding; don't try to make your spouse into a revised edition of yourself. Look at your differences as creative strengths, not as marks of inferiority.

In many marriages one spouse considers his beliefs, traditions, and behaviors to be superior to those of the other spouse. "You do things differently than I do. You like your meat fixed differently than I do. Therefore

6. Olthius, James H. *I Pledge You My Troth*, New York: 1975, pp. 112-113.

you must be wrong." Why must we equate differentness with inferiority or being wrong? Why must we demand that our spouse do things exactly as we do, or say exactly the same words with the same number of sentences as we do when disciplining the kids? Your spouse did not marry you so that you could pass judgment on him or her!

Ephesians 4:2 says, "Living as becomes you—with complete lowliness of mind (humility) and meekness (unselfishness, gentleness, mildness), with patience, bearing with one another and making allowances because you love one another" (Amplified). Perhaps "making allowances because you love one another" means that you can allow your partner to think with a different form of logic than you employ, to hold some beliefs different from yours, to clean the house or arrange work spaces differently than you would. And this does not mean that your mate is wrong or is inferior to you.

You have probably heard of, or even experienced, examples of conflict because marriage partners cannot or will not accept different behaviors. A husband wants the salad dressing poured over the whole salad before it is brought to the table, while his wife wants it poured over the individual servings. One spouse prefers to have the toilet paper roll off from the bottom of the roll while the other prefers the top; each day they switch the roll if it is not set up according to their preference. A man who worked in a dust-free lab as a technician was married to a very neat woman. But he required that the house be so immaculate that he brought home a four thousand dollar dust analysis machine from work and set it up in the living room to measure the dust content. Another husband drew up blueprints for his wife to follow; they plotted the exact way she was to vacuum each room of the house, how she was to wash and wipe the dishes, and so on. He did this because he felt that she was wasting time and energy doing the housework in her own style. He demanded that she follow his pattern. She kept to it for four months; then she got tired of the pressure and left him for a while so he could get the message that he ought to back off!

Isn't it interesting that the very uniqueness which attracted us to the one that we married becomes an irritant, and we seek both openly and subtly to modify the things that make the partner different.

Why not spend as much time and effort trying to understand your spouse's viewpoint and life style as you spend trying to make him or her understand yours? Everyone's background and environment is different, and they bring the differences with them to the marriage. Paul Tournier said, "Few people really accept the fact that their marital partner behaves in a profoundly different way from themselves. yet how often you hear them say, 'I cannot understand my husband' or 'I cannot understand my wife.' The 'I cannot understand' really means 'I cannot understand that my husband is different from me, that he thinks, feels, and acts is different from me, that he thinks, feels, and acts in a quite different manner than me.[7]' " If you were to ask your spouse why he does what he does, he might not be able to explain; he might not even know himself. Maybe through mutual discussion you can both come to understand—and build your relationship at the same time.

This is not to say that there will not be legitimate complaints on your part; there will be, and these ought to be expressed to your partner. But ask yourself if the changes which you seek are for the good of your spouse and the relationship, or if they are just personal preference. You can discuss areas of personal preference and share the reasons for the change you desire; your

7. Tournier, Paul. *To Understand Each Other.* Richmond, Va.: John Knox Press, 1967, pp. 21-22.

partner can then choose to comply or not to comply, and can give reasons. But the happiness of your marriage is not really based upon these changes. We can learn to live with differences! We *must* learn to live with them.

Be forewarned about change: even when you've asked for it, you will have to adjust to it. If one partner makes a major change in his or her marital behavior, in the style of interaction, or in an area of responsibility, this could actually be disruptive to the marriage if the other partner doesn't make some changes as well. A woman, who was married to an alcoholic for many years, found herself greatly depressed and upset for some time after her husband stopped drinking and turned his life around. She was so used to responding to an alcoholic that she had not considered what it would be like to live with a sober husband. She had to completely alter her thinking pattern about him and the way she acted toward him.

A wife who wanted her husband to become more involved with the rearing of the children, handle the finances, and make more decisions around the house was quite taken aback when I mentioned that if he did all these things she, too, would have to make many changes. I asked, "When your husband begins to do all of these things, which he has now said that he will do, are you going to allow him to do them according to his temperament and his style, and at his rate? Or have you already decided how he is to discipline the children, handle the bookwork, and make decisions? He will probably do it his way. Had you thought about that? Are you going to be able to adjust to that, and not tell him how to do it?"

She said that she had never considered that part of it. She had just assumed that she could continue responding to him as she always had. But it doesn't work that way. Before you seek out a change on the part of your mate, consider what it will cost you in terms of adjustment.

And remember—if you would like to see some changes on the part of your mate, it can be accomplished. If you will make changes in your own life your spouse will probably change and behave differently in relationship to the changes that he sees in you.

Arrange with your spouse a time when you can sit down together without the possibility of interruptions. Read the following quotes together, out loud. Then each of you should tell how *you* see each quotation relating to your own life and how it could affect your response as a marriage partner.

"Every marriage is like a set of fingerprints with its own unique pattern. Each spouse begins with certain ideas and preferences that may be subject to the influence or pressure of the other. To have an opinion, to believe in something, is natural to all of us. But we need to be flexible, for our personal views may not be the right or only ones. We must accept difference, even to the point of understanding that what seems to be an infuriating contrast in views can ultimately be an asset.[8]"

"In the midst of the marital struggle the honeymoon dream vanishes, and the despair over the old relationship comes up for reexamination. Suddenly each spouse turns his eyes away from the partner, and looks inwardly and asks 'What am I doing to my partner? What is wrong with me? What am I misunderstanding? What must I do to rescue this marriage?' If honestly asked the answers are not far behind: 'I really married my wife because of her difference. It is not my job to make her over, but rather to discover and to value that difference. But before I can do that I must accept my difference and I really need her to help me discover my uniqueness. My task is not to mold her into a beautiful vase, but to participate with her to discover that beauti-

8. Lobenz, Norman M. and Clark W. Blackburn. *How to Stay Married.* New York: Cowles Book Co., 1968, p. 66.

ful vase, even as we discover it in me. How arrogant of me to think I could shape another human being! How humble it makes me to realize that I need to yield to another and thereby be changed. Our relationship will change both of us—in a process of being shaped into a form far more beautiful than either could imagine.[9]"

"The difference makes the difference. Unless there can be a give and take, a mutual sharing, unless two people have something to offer each other while receiving something in return, what is the use in being married? It is not in the areas of similarities, it is in the areas of difference, the contrasts, the unlikeness, that the benefits of marriage accrue. There is someone in this world who is the perfect counterpart of your every need, who is strong everywhere you are weak, and who has an asset everywhere you have a liability.[10]"

After discussing the quotations, complete the following discussion guide. Go over it with your spouse after each of you has completed it. (Write your answers on separate pieces of paper so you are not influenced by seeing your mate's answers.)

9. Schmitt, Abraham. *Conflict and Ecstasy.* Printed manuscript.

10. Bisagno, John R. *Love is Something You Do.* New York: Harper & Row, 1975, p. 13.

1. Write down several ways in which you and your spouse are alike.
2. Write down several ways in which you and your spouse are different.
3. For each item you just listed, indicate how it affects you. Do you like or dislike it? Then indicate how each item affects the marriage relationship.
4. If any of the items have had a hindering effect on the marriage, indicate in what way this has occurred. Then try to decide how this could be turned into an asset for the marriage.
5. Write down five of your strengths which help the marriage.
6. Write down five of your spouse's strengths which help the marriage.
7. Which of your own behaviors would you like to change in order to enrich your marriage?
8. In what way could your spouse help you in making any of these changes?

Discover and implement the scriptural pattern of husband and wife relationships— SERVANTHOOD! Identify and mutually assign areas of competence and responsibility in the marital relationship.

Failure to clarify the husband-wife roles in a relationship is a major cause of marital disruption. As a couple you are involved in an almost endless number of activities and responsibilities. Each couple should discuss and decide who is most competent to do which task. Assignment of tasks should not be made simply because of parental example, because it is expected in your social group, or because of tradition. When a couple's or an individual's abilities, training and temperament make it difficult or unnecessary to follow an established cultural norm for a role, they may need to have the strength to establish their own style of working together as a couple. It is imperative that a couple deliberately and mutually develop rules and guidelines for their relationship as husband and wife. This clear assignment of authority and responsibility by the spouses does not create a rigid relationship but allows flexibility and order in what could become a chaotic mess.

Let's spend some time now thinking about your role as a wife or a husband. You will need a good block of time to work through the following questions and evaluation forms. Be sure you write out all of your answers individually before discussing your responses together.

First complete the following sentences and discuss them.

In marriage I believe a "role" is . . .

My main role in marriage is . . .

I began to form this belief about my role when . . .

My mate's role is . . .

In marriage a wife should . . .

In marriage a husband should . . .

I can best help my mate fulfill his or her role by . . .

TRADITIONAL MASCULINE ROLES

We all have certain basic ideas of the roles men should play in marriage. List here five basic roles that are usually expected of married men in our society.

1. _______________________________________
2. _______________________________________
3. _______________________________________
4. _______________________________________
5. _______________________________________

Now be creative. Think of four new roles that men might play in marriage—roles that are not included in the traditional masculine ideal. They might be roles a man can carry out at home with his children, on the job, or in the community. Try to think of roles that help a man to realize his potential, that contribute to a fuller expression of his personality.

1. _______________________________________
2. _______________________________________
3. _______________________________________
4. _______________________________________

TRADITIONAL FEMININE ROLES

Focus your attention on the traditional feminine roles in marriage. List below five roles that are usually expected of married women in our society.

1. _______________________________________
2. _______________________________________
3. _______________________________________
4. _______________________________________
5. _______________________________________

Next, be creative. Think of four new roles that women might play in marriage—roles that are not included in the traditional feminine ideal. Include new roles in the business world, in the community, in politics, and at home. Try to think of roles that broaden a woman's range of interest and activities and encourage her self-expression.

1. _______________________________________
2. _______________________________________
3. _______________________________________
4. _______________________________________

SHARED ROLES

Great emphasis is being placed on shared role behavior in contemporary marriage. Many of the daily tasks of marriage can be shared by husband and wife. List below four roles that you saw your parents share or that you have observed other couples sharing.

1. _______________________________________
2. _______________________________________
3. _______________________________________
4. _______________________________________

List four roles that you are now sharing in your own marriage.

1. _______________________________________
2. _______________________________________
3. _______________________________________
4. _______________________________________

Use a separate piece of paper for the Role Concepts Comparison that follows. Read each statement and write down the appropriate number indicating what you believe about each one. Then go back and indicate how you think your spouse responded to each statement. Next indicate with a "yes" or a "no" whether *your belief* about the statement is *actually* in practice in your home at the present time. Finally, write down for each one where you obtained your belief—from your parents, pastor, friends, your own idea.

After each of you has completed the form sit down together and share your responses. Perhaps the husband could start; choosing any statement, read it aloud and then say, "This is how I answered the statement, and this is how I think you answered it." Then the wife can share her responses and you can discuss your answers together.

Remember to consider whether you would like to change any of these beliefs or behaviors. They may be satisfactory or they may not; this is your opportunity to discuss them and devise a new plan.

YOUR ROLE CONCEPTS COMPARISON

What do you believe about your role concept in marriage?
Circle: (1) strongly agree
        (2) mildly agree
        (3) not sure
        (4) mildly disagree
        (5) strongly disagree

Wife   *Husband*

1 2 3 4 5 The husband is the   1 2 3 4 5
          head of the home.

Wife *Husband*

1 2 3 4 5 The wife should not be employed outside the home.   1 2 3 4 5

1 2 3 4 5 The husband should help regularly with the dishes.   1 2 3 4 5

1 2 3 4 5 The wife has the greater responsibility for the children.   1 2 3 4 5

1 2 3 4 5 Money that the wife earns is her money.   1 2 3 4 5

1 2 3 4 5 The husband should have at least one night a week out with his friends.   1 2 3 4 5

1 2 3 4 5 The wife should always be the one to cook.   1 2 3 4 5

1 2 3 4 5 The husband's responsibility is to his job and the wife's responsibility is to the home and children.   1 2 3 4 5

Wife   *Husband*

1 2 3 4 5   Money can best be handled through a joint checking account.   1 2 3 4 5

1 2 3 4 5   Marriage is a 50-50 proposition.   1 2 3 4 5

1 2 3 4 5   Major decisions should be made by the husband in case of an impasse.   1 2 3 4 5

1 2 3 4 5   The husband should babysit one night a week so the wife can get away and do what she wants.   1 2 3 4 5

1 2 3 4 5   A couple should spend their recreation leisure activities with one another.   1 2 3 4 5

1 2 3 4 5   It is all right for the wife to initiate love-making with her husband.   1 2 3 4 5

Wife   *Husband*

1 2 3 4 5 The husband and   1 2 3 4 5
wife should plan the
budget and manage
money matters
together.

1 2 3 4 5 Neither the husband   1 2 3 4 5
or wife should
purchase an item cost-
ing more than fifteen
dollars without con-
sulting the other.

1 2 3 4 5 The father is the one   1 2 3 4 5
responsible for dis-
cipling the children.

1 2 3 4 5 A wife who has   1 2 3 4 5
special talent should
have a career.

1 2 3 4 5 It is the wife's   1 2 3 4 5
responsibility to have
the house neat and
clean.

1 2 3 4 5 Arguments are a   1 2 3 4 5
definite part of
marriage.

Wife   *Husband*

1 2 3 4 5 The husband should take his wife out somewhere twice a month. 1 2 3 4 5

1 2 3 4 5 The wife is just as responsible for the children's discipline as the husband. 1 2 3 4 5
1 2 3 4 5

1 2 3 4 5 It is the husband's job to do the yard work. 1 2 3 4 5

1 2 3 4 5 The mother should be the teacher of values to the children. 1 2 3 4 5

1 2 3 4 5 Women are more emotional than men. 1 2 3 4 5

1 2 3 4 5 Children should be allowed to help plan family activities. 1 2 3 4 5

1 2 3 4 5 Children develop better in a home with parents who are strict disciplinarians. 1 2 3 4 5

Wife						Husband				
1	2	3	4	5	The wife should always obey what her husband asks her to do.	1	2	3	4	5
1	2	3	4	5	The husband should decide which areas each should be responsible for.	1	2	3	4	5
1	2	3	4	5	Neither husband or wife should bring their parents into the home to live.	1	2	3	4	5
1	2	3	4	5	Quarrels are always wrong in marriage relationships.	1	2	3	4	5
1	2	3	4	5	It is better to modify the truth to avoid unpleasant situations in the family.	1	2	3	4	5

In addition to roles and responsibilities, decision-making is a part of marriage. Who makes the decisions in your relationship? How much influence do you have in some of the crucial areas? Here is your opportunity to determine your influence in decision-making. Use the following outline, following the instructions and writing your answers on a separate piece of paper. After both of you have done this, exchange papers, compare your answers, and discuss the results together.

One main question to consider is this: Is each of us making decisions in the areas where he or she is the most gifted? Does each person have sufficient opportunity to give what he or she has to offer? What is the reason for one or the other having the percentage of influence that is evident?

YOUR PERCENTAGE OF THE DECISION

Describe the decision-making process of your marriage by putting the percentage of influence you have, and your spouse has, for various issues. The total for each decision must be 100%. (Those who put 50:50 too many times will be considered dishonest.)

	My Vote	Spouse's Vote
Choice of new car	___	___
Choice of home	___	___
Choice of furniture	___	___
Choice of your own wardrobe	___	___

	My Vote	Spouse's Vote
Choice of vacation spots	___	___
Choice of decor for the home ...	___	___
Choice of mutual friends	___	___
Choice of entertainment	___	___
Choice of church	___	___
Choice of child rearing practices	___	___
Choice of TV shows	___	___
Choice of home menu	___	___
Choice of number of children ...	___	___
Choice of where we live........	___	___
Choice of husband's vocation ...	___	___
Choice of wife's vocation	___	___
Choice of determining for what and how the money is spent ..	___	___

(Place checks by the issues that are not presently satisfactory to you.)

Now that you have completed the assigned work concerning your responsibilities and your husband-wife roles, what are you thinking?

Perhaps this approach is not what you were expecting. You may have read other books on husband-wife roles in which the discussion focused primarily on Ephesians 5:21-23 and I Peter 3:1-8, in which the emphasis is upon the wife being submissive to her husband and the husband being the head of the wife. This teaching of God's Word must be understood properly. All too often the stress is placed totally upon the wife being submissive and the husband being the leader, with implications that the husband is the only decision-maker and that the wife must be at home and must not seek a career in order to develop her giftedness.

In contrast, consider what the following two authors suggest concerning the husband-wife role:

"The principle of mutuality of submissiveness in marriage is similar to the pattern of submissiveness between the members of the body of Christ. There are times in the body when it is appropriate for one member to exercise leadership over the other members as a function of his or her spiritual gift (I Corinthians 12:14-26). No single spiritual gift automatically qualifies a member to be the leader or ultimate decision-maker all of the time. That position belongs to the head, Jesus Himself. Likewise in marriage, in which there is mutuality of submission, the role of leadership is assigned not according to some decree from God, or on the basis of "maleness" or "femaleness," but on the basis of the leadership role the partner has been assigned by the mutual decision of the marriage. The skill of a Christian marriage lies in the negotiation and assignment of these leadership roles on the basis of the abilities of the partners.[11]"

"In the marriage the husband has the office of head. That simply means he has the responsibility and authority to call the marriage—his wife as well as himself—to obey the norm of troth. If he faithfully exercises his office, both he and his wife will be freed to be themselves. As the head, the husband is called to take the lead in mutually examining the marriage to see if it is developing according to its long-range goals.

"Clearly, headship has nothing to do with being boss. The husband can only command the wife to live up to what the two of them mutually pledged when they married. Likewise, if the husband neglects his office, the wife ought to call the husband back to their mutual vows.

"Neither does headship imply inferiority or superiority. Rather, headship is a special office of service so that the marriage may thrive and grow. Headship does not mean that the husband leads or decides in every detail. Once a man and woman have decided which vision of life is going to norm their activities in their marriage, they can leave

11. Guernsey, Dennis. *Thoroughly Married*. Waco, Texas: Word Books, 1976.

the decisions in day-to-day affairs to the partner with the appropriate talents, temperaments, and situations. The husband's unique role is to be on guard continually so that the 'little' things do not develop into the kinds of patterns that undermine the entire marriage.[12] "

Too many husbands and wives are caught up in the game of checking up on their spouses to see if they are performing the proper scriptural role. Let's try a more positive approach instead. If you're going to build your marriage in accord with scripture, what should your emphasis be? Here are several ideas for you to consider.

1. Pay attention to the scripture portions directed at *yourself;* seek to live these out in your own life regardless of what your spouse is doing. Seek to put the scripture into your life not for what it might do for your spouse and how it might change him or her, but simply because God has said this is the best way for you to live.

2. Decision-making and roles within marriage should be based upon the giftedness of the individuals and their uniqueness, and not on prescribed roles others have set up for the Christian community of married couples.

3. The husband, according to scripture, is

12. Olthius, p. 27.

responsible for setting the tone of the home. He is a stabilizing factor and should take the initiative in the spiritual and emotional development of family members. His role is not that of a dictator but that of a self-sacrificing servant.

The main role of the husband is that of servanthood. The scripture in Ephesians 5 gives Christ as the example for the husband. It states that He loved the church and gave Himself for her that He might sanctify her and present her to Himself in glory. A husband is to nourish and cherish his wife as he does his own body. Peter adds that he is to be understanding of her and to give her honor. What do some of these words and concepts mean? The word "nourish" means to give someone an abundance of what she needs to flourish and develop. It isn't just giving the bare necessities so that she remains alive: it is giving the best enrichment for her growth.

What does "understanding" mean? It means that a husband is willing to listen to his wife's point of view. He is willing to think with her. He is sensitive to her feelings and moods and tries to discover her needs in order to meet them. He knows when to take her out to dinner to escape a case of insanity brought on by three preschool kids! He treats his wife with respect, love and consideration, and endeavors to protect her from hurtful situations. He is compelled because of this love to respond to every claim the wife may make for support, sympathy, protection of happiness.

If the husband would practice his God-given role as a self-sacrificing servant, it would serve as a practical example to other members of the family. They, too, would learn to love and serve.

Unfortunately, in so many homes it has been the wife who has been the most self-sacrificing member of the family. She has given and adapted and adjusted to meet the husband's needs. Why shouldn't the husband, in being the leader of the home, set the example for sacrificial love? In place of having the home structured around him and his schedule and needs, let him help develop a home life. If he can take the initiative in this, then both partners can work together in meeting each other's needs.

Try to discover the unique needs of your mate and to meet these needs through positive behaviors and comments.

One of the main reasons that you married your spouse was to have your needs met. But does your spouse know specifically what your needs are and how to meet them? Do you know what his or her needs are? Better yet, do you know what your own needs are? If you ask another person to meet your needs and you cannot explain what they are or how to meet them, the other person can hardly be blamed for not meeting them.

One of the questions I ask couples who come for premarital counseling is, "When you are sick do you like a lot of attention or do you prefer being left alone?" Most couples look at one another and say that they had never considered that question. And yet it is important when it comes to meeting needs. In most cases one states that he prefers being left alone, while the other was planning to wait on the sick partner hand and foot! Discussing this prior to marriage can avert a potential conflict and hurt feelings.

What can a husband do to meet the needs of his wife? Even though this varies from couple to couple, there are several very simple but crucial behaviors that a husband can perform that will definitely encourage and help his spouse. These are concerns that have been shared in counseling by several hundred couples over the past two years. These are what wives feel are very important to them.

1. When you come home at night, greet your wife with affection and a question or

comment which focuses on what her day was like. Don't pet the dog first or ask for the mail without some contact with your wife.

2. Be willing to listen without doing another task at the same time. Talk to her without having the TV on; be willing to turn it off to talk with her.

3. Be affectionate and caring on days when you aren't wanting sexual intercourse.

4. When you communicate, give your wife details of the event or story. Communicate with her on an emotional level, sharing your feelings and responding to her emotions.

And what of the wife's role? Betty Coble, in her excellent book *Woman—Aware and Choosing*, discusses ways that a wife communicates rejection to her husband. In considering how a wife meets her husband's needs, consider the following types of behavior which definitely *do not* meet his needs!

1. Arguing with him when he has already made a decision.

2. Questioning the importance of his role as the father; criticizing the way he handles his role.

3. Disagreeing with him in the presence of others.

4. Parading his past failures as a leader.

5. Insulting him by talking about 'going

back to work,' so she could have some of the things she wants, or because she is so unfulfilled.

6. Expressing no pleasure with his gifts to her.

7. Not realizing that he has a need to achieve and that much of his self-concept is tied in with his work.

8. Not giving recognition to what he is doing right; paying maximum attention to what is wrong with what he is doing.

Here is a helpful way of looking at the meeting of needs for spouses. Read the following material and complete the instructions that are given at the end.

Years ago a psychologist named Abraham Maslow suggested that each person has certain basic needs in his or her life. He listed these needs in order of their importance. First, a person seeks to fulfill his physiological needs. These are those things that are necessary in order to sustain life: food, water, oxygen, rest, etc. Second, a person seeks to fulfill safety needs, which involve the need for a safe environment, protection from harm, etc. Third, after having the first two sets of needs fulfilled, a person seeks to fulfill his or her need for love and belonging. This includes a desire for affectionate relationships with others. Fourth, a person seeks to fulfill his or her need for esteem. Esteem involves receiving recognition as a worthwhile person. Finally, after the other levels of needs are met, a person seeks to fulfill the need of self-actualization. This is the need to become the person one has the potential to become.

MASLOW'S LEVELS OF NEEDS

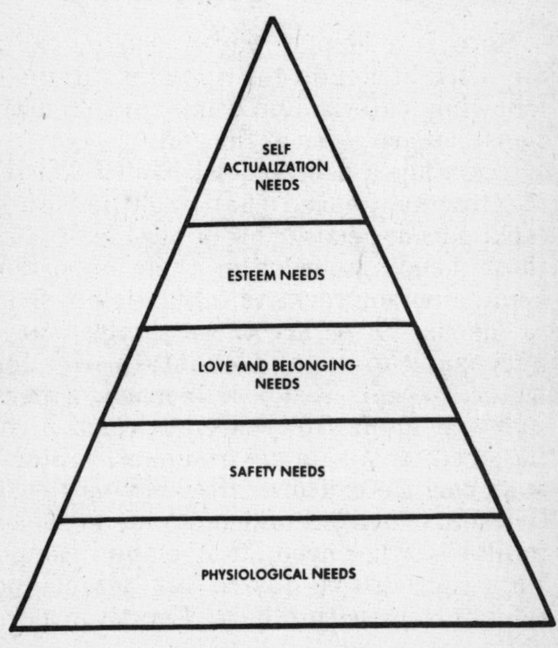

Most husbands and wives help to fulfill the first two levels of needs in one another—the physiological and safety needs. Most husbands, for example, allow their wives sufficient air, water, food, and rest. And most are concerned about keeping the car in good running order, making sure the house is safe with proper lighting, ventilation, locks, and so on. But where most husbands and wives fall down is in meeting their spouses' needs for love and belonging, esteem, and self-actualization.

Looking at the chart of the hierarchy of needs, complete these sentences:

1. During the coming week the way in which I will try to meet the needs of my spouse in the last three areas is . . .

2. The way in which my spouse can best meet my own needs for love, esteem and self-actualization is . . .

Discuss your answers with your spouse. You may find that you are already doing what you should be; or you may discover some surprises. One husband wrote that to build his wife's esteem he would give her at least one compliment a day, and each week would endeavor to give her some new compliment that she had never received before. Another husband said that he would babysit one night a week so his wife could take art lessons or work on completing her college degree. A wife stated that she took a course in stocks and bonds so she could communicate more effectively with her stock broker husband. A husband said that he would encourage his wife to pursue a career that she was interested in, as she was very gifted and could fulfill the role of a homemaker and have a career simultaneously.

Sharing your specific needs and how to fulfill them with your spouse does not mean that the romance has gone out of your relationship. Your marriage will be enhanced because of this new knowledge of one another. You can seek to meet needs openly and honestly without the misunderstanding or manipulation that can creep into some of our responses.

Some couples have taken the time to write lists of actions which were important to them. These were things that they would like their spouse to do for them. After sharing the lists together, each partner made it a project to put the actions into practice. Here is a sample list from one couple:

The husband's requests: "Wash my back; fix the orange juice; call me at work; invite me to expose the details of my work; touch me when I drive; hold me when you see that I'm down; tell me about your experiences at work each day."

The wife's requests: "Ask me what record I would like to hear and put it on; tell me you love me; tell me when I look attractive; look at me when I'm telling you something; if you're going to stop at the store for something, ask me if there is anything that I want; put your things away when you come in; greet me with a hug and kiss in the morning before we get out of bed; ask my opinion about things you write."

You and your spouse should now complete the following evaluation individually; then share your answers with one another.

A. Please list ten things which your spouse does which please you.

1. _______________________________________
2. _______________________________________
3. _______________________________________
4. _______________________________________
5. _______________________________________
6. _______________________________________
7. _______________________________________
8. _______________________________________
9. _______________________________________
10. ______________________________________

B. Please list five things which you would like your spouse to do *more often*. Be *positive* and *specific*. How often did he or she do each of these things in the last week? How important are each of these things to you?

1. _______________________________________

It was done _____________ times in the last week.
Do you consider it:
- [ ] very important
- [ ] important
- [ ] not too important

2. _______________________________________

It was done _____________ times in the last week.
Do you consider it:
- [ ] very important
- [ ] important
- [ ] not too important

3. _______________________________________

It was done _____________ times in the last week.
Do you consider it:
- [ ] very important
- [ ] important
- [ ] not too important

4. ______________________________________

It was done ________________ times in the last week.
Do you consider it:
- ☐ very important
- ☐ important
- ☐ not too important

5. ______________________________________

It was done ________________ times in the last week.
Do you consider it:
- ☐ very important
- ☐ important
- ☐ not too important

C. Please list five things which your spouse would like you to do *more often*, again being positive and specific.
How often have you done each of these in the last week? About how often has your spouse asked you to do each of these things during the last week?

1. ______________________________________

I did it ________________ times in the last week.
My spouse asked me to do this ________________ times in the last week.

2. ______________________________________

I did it ___________________ times in the last week.
My spouse asked me to do this ______________ times in the last week.

3. ______________________________________

I did it___________________ times in the last week.
My spouse asked me to do this ______________ times in the last week.

4. ______________________________________

I did it ___________________ times in the last week.
My spouse asked me to do this ______________ times in the last week.

5. ______________________________________

I did it ___________________ times in the last week.
My spouse asked me to do this ______________ times in the last week.[13]

13. Adapted from the Marital Pre-Counseling Inventory. Research Press, Champaign, Ill.

This book would not be complete if the two most important factors in a successful marriage were not mentioned. Space permits them to be mentioned but not to be amplified here. Each of them would take a complete book in itself to be of assistance.

Your own self-concept and your ability to communicate effectively will make possible all of the steps to a better marriage discussed in this book.

Your self-concept is the image that you have of yourself. It is the mental picture that you have of what you are like; it is the sensation of being somebody. If you have an adequate self-concept you feel good and positive about yourself. If not, you have an insecurity which can make a marriage shaky and which is the basis for most of the worry, depression and anger that you experience. If you need help here, you might read *The Sensation of Being Somebody* by Dr. Maurice Wagner (Zondervan) and *Do I Have to Be Me?* by Dr. Lloyd Ahlem (Regal).

Communication—what can be said about it? You cannot have a relationship unless you can communicate adequately. We all communicate, but much of our communication is destructive and superficial. Here is what some have said about the subject:

"Communication is to love what blood is to the body.[14] "

"Communication is essential to the expression of love and indeed to life itself. Where there is love, there must be communication, because love can never be passive and inactive. Love inevitably expresses itself and moves out toward others. When communication breaks down, love is blocked and its energy will turn to resentment and hostility.[15] "

"If there is any indispensable insight with which a young married couple should begin their life together, it is that they should try to keep open, at all cost, the lines of communication between them.[16] "

"Love is the opening of one's life to another in intimate, understanding communication. When two persons can share from the very center of their existence, they experience love in its truest quality. Marriage is a venture into intimacy, and intimacy is the opening of oneself to another.[17] "

14. Howe, Reuel. *The Miracle of Dialogue.* New York: Seabury Press, 1963, p. 3.

15. Howe, p. 99.

16. Howe, Reuel. *Herein Is Love.* Valley Forge, Pa.: Judson Press, 1961, p. 100.

17. Augsburger, David. *Cherishable: Love and Marriage.* Scottsdale, Pa.: Herald Press, 1971, pp. 16, 55.

For your reading and study regarding communication, obtain the following books: *Communication—Key to Your Marriage* by H. Norman Wright (Regal) and *Family Communication* by Sven Wahlroos (Macmillan).

If you have followed the instructions in this book you have evaluated your marriage. You may have found areas of concern, or you may have been pleasantly surprised. To keep your marriage growing you must continually work at it. If you don't it will probably regress; or indifference may set in with all its negative effects. You have too much to gain in your marriage to neglect it. If your spouse is not as eager as you to enhance the marriage, do not attack or criticize him or her, and don't give up. Keep working and maturing as an individual and continue to encourage your partner.

Perhaps the basis for a good marriage relationship can be found in this passage from Philippians. Ask yourself how this can be put into practice in your marriage. What will be the results of acting upon this teaching from the Word?

"Do nothing from factional motives—through contentiousness, strife, selfishness or for unworthy ends—or prompted by conceit and empty arrogance. Instead, in the true spirit of humility (lowliness of mind) let each regard the others as better than and superior to himself—thinking more highly of one another than you do of yourselves.

"Let each of you esteem and look upon and be concerned for not (merely) his own interests, but also each for the interests of others" (Philippians 2:3-4).

STUDY AND DISCUSSION IDEAS

AGREE-DISAGREE

WHAT DO YOU THINK?

The following statements are intended to provoke thought. Read each one and decide whether you agree or disagree with it. Mark the appropriate space to indicate your response.

If you are using this book in a class, duplicate a copy of the *Agree-Disagree* sheet for each person. Ask the class members to complete the form. Then go through the questions one-by-one and ask for a show of hands to indicate who agreed and who disagreed. Discuss further those questions which brought the most divided response from the group.

Agree Disagree   Statement

_______ _______ 1. The Bible teaches that the husband is the head of the home. He should stand up for his own opinion and expect obedience from his wife.

_______ _______ 2. The father in the home actually has more influence upon the children than the mother.

_______ _______ 3. If we are married and our mate does something that bothers us, we should go ahead and tell him or her and try to change it.

_______ _______ 4. The husband's primary responsibility is to his job and the wife's primary responsibility is to the home and the children.

_______ _______ 5. Marriage is a 50-50 proposition.

The following questions can be used for further discussion with couples or in small groups. Each person should give his or her initial response to the question and then the couple or the group should continue to discuss the answers.

1. State *your* definition of marriage.
2. Describe your marriage using five adjectives.
3. How do you think your spouse would describe your marriage?
4. What expectations does God have for your marriage?
5. How has your marriage developed in a positive way since you were first married?
6. Do you try to change your mate or yourself more when differences arise? In what ways?
7. Who do you feel is the more dominant in your marriage? How is this demonstrated?
8. Describe one goal that you have for your marriage.
9. Describe your marriage as you experienced it during the first year.
10. How would your mate describe your marriage to your friends?
11. Describe the funniest thing that ever happened to you in your marriage.
12. Who exerts most of the influence over finances in your home? Why?

13. Describe what you can do to demonstrate these two verses in your marriage:

> "Let each of you esteem and look upon and be concerned for not (merely) his own interests, but also each for the interests of others." (Phil. 2:4)

> "Living as becomes you—with complete lowliness of mind (humility) and meekness (unselfishness, gentleness, mildness), with patience, bearing with one another and making allowances because you love one another." (Eph. 4:2)

14. In what way has marriage given you freedom?

15. Since marriage, the following changes have taken place in our relationship:

16. If my spouse could change one thing about me it would be:

17. If I could change one thing about my spouse it would be:

18. In what way could you be a better listener?

19. How does your spouse show you that he or she is really listening to you when you are speaking?

20. Face your spouse and complete this statement: "What I appreciate about you is: "

21. Describe a recent disagreement. What did you do to resolve it?

22. What is the best way that you settle differences in your marriage?
23. My mate and I have some differences over:
24. I feel most like communicating with my partner when:
25. List four things that your partner does which make it difficult to share yourself with him or her.
26. Is it hard to understand your spouse's feelings and attitudes? Why? Why not?
27. In what ways does your spouse try to lift your spirits when you are depressed or discouraged?
28. When was the first time you were aware that your spouse loved you?
29. When you get upset, how do you show it?
30. Can you tell if your spouse is upset? How?
31. List three things about your partner's parents that you really like.
32. As far as our marriage is concerned, our in-laws need to learn:
33. If you could ask Jesus to change one thing about your marriage, what would it be?
34. Is it easy for you and your spouse to pray together? Why or why not?
35. As I pray for my spouse this week, I will pray for: